IFOR HIGGON'S
CAMBRIAN
DIARY

Ex-GWR 'Mogul' No. 5331 leaves the loop at Garneddwen Summit with the 9.00am 'Saturdays Only' Paddington to Pwllheli through train on 1st June 1956. The platforms of Garneddwen Halt can be seen by the rear of the train, a fairly uniform rake of carmine and cream liveried stock. The halt was opened by the GWR on 9th July 1928 and closed with the line on 18th January 1965, although services over the whole route were severely disrupted during the final week due to damage caused by flooding near Llanderfel which, with closure imminent, was not worth repairing. The staggered platforms here were only accesible by a path from the nearby Bala-Dolgellau road (now the A494).

IFOR HIGGON'S CAMBRIAN DIARY

GWYN BRIWNANT JONES

The epitome of the Great Western on the Cambrian in the late 1930s. The coaches were in good order and could range from recently out-shopped and immaculate Edwardian clerestories to newly introduced Collett 'Sunshine' stock (so called because of the large windows which allowed more light in to the carriage), hauled by the 'Duke' Class 4-4-0s hastily introduced as a stop-gap measure in 1936. No. 3259 *Merlin*, built in September 1895, originally running as No. 3260 and a long time favourite of Cambrian enginemen, is seen at the head of the 10.10am from Pwllheli to Dovey Junction on 7th June 1938. Immediately behind the engine is one of the aforementioned Collett coaches, with its distinctive 'high waist', which had recently been introduced to the area. Locomotive and coach present something of a poignant juxtaposition, as *Merlin*'s time in service was approaching its end, withdrawal occurring four months after the picture was taken, in October 1938. However, in the following month, parts of the engine, including the cab, were used in the construction of 'Dukedog' No. 3221, which was built on the frames of 'Bulldog' No. 3411.

CONTENTS

ACKNOWLEDGEMENTS

I am grateful to Lightmoor Press for agreeing to take on and publish this tribute to Ifor Higgons, which in some small way serves to acknowledge his talents as a photographer. Neil Parkhouse has provided additional information for the captions, whilst John Lewis has cast his knowledgeable eye over the coaching stock featured in many of the pictures and his notes thus add further to our enjoyment and understanding of Ifor's work. Finally, my thanks must go as well to Stephen Phillips, who compiled a few notes to assist in keeping us 'on track' with the Vale of Rheidol photograph.

Published by LIGHTMOOR PRESS
© Lightmoor Press & Gwyn Briwnant Jones 2018
Designed by Neil Parkhouse

LIGHTMOOR PRESS
Unit 144B, Lydney Trading Estate, Harbour Road, Lydney, Gloucestershire GL15 4EJ
www.lightmoor.co.uk
Lightmoor Press is an imprint of Black Dwarf Lightmoor Publications Ltd

Printed in England by Henry Ling Ltd, The Dorset Press, Dorchester
www.henryling.co.uk

PREFACE

Compilation of this brief tribute to the late Ifor Higgon has been a pleasant task, working from his archive of well over 1,000 negatives, all taken between 1924 and 1967. Although Ifor undoubtedly derived great pleasure from assembling this collection, somewhat surprisingly perhaps, he appears not to have devoted much attention to printing them up, being content from quite an early date to rely on standard commercial processing for his proof prints. He was always hard working and fully occupied assisting his father with various building and repair projects for the company he worked for, Solomon Andrews & Son. Thus, it was almost as though he put photographic processing to one side, that he might enjoy the task more fully in later life when he would have more time to devote to it.

Only after he had met the late C.C. Green MBE in the post-war years, and allowed him to borrow the negatives, can he have had an accurate view of the strength of his archive. Higgon and Green approached the task meticulously and Ifor made a series of wooden boxes into which the glass photographic plates were slotted. These were loaned to Green, in sequence, for transportation to Birmingham for printing, then duly exchanged for further batches as the work progressed. The two men co-operated in harmonious fashion, resulting in the production of a fine legacy of Cambrian line images.

The provision of adequate motive power on the Cambrian main line was an urgent requirement during the first years after the Grouping. Although the civil engineer made all possible haste with the strengthening and re-laying of the permanent way, the initial solution was to draft in examples of the older 'Dean Goods' and 'Duke' classes. Admittedly, they had been put through the works at Swindon before despatch to central Wales and they were obviously early candidates for Ifor Higgon's camera, as the photographs within these pages show. The late 1930s witnessed the introduction of the 'Earl' Class 4-4-0s – or 'Dukedogs' as they were more commonly known – matched to GWR coaching stock in good order. No. 3205 was photographed at Barmouth Junction with the 5.15pm working from Pwllheli to Machynlleth on 16th July 1937. Ifor noted on the rear of the print that the engine's *Earl of Devon* nameplates had recently been removed. The 'Dukedogs' were mongrels, built on the frames of scrapped 'Bulldogs' using parts from scrapped 'Dukes', for which they were regarded as replacements. No. 3205 utilised the frames of No. 3413 *James Mason* but replaced No. 3255 *Excaliber*. It was withdrawn from Oswestry shed in July 1959 as No. 9005, having been renumbered in 1946 as the '32xx' series was reallocated for use on new Collett Class '22xx' 0-6-0s.

INTRODUCTION

Ifor Aneurin Higgon was born in Llangelynin, Merioneth, on 22nd May 1908 and brought up in the family home at 1 Glasfryn Terrace, the end property of a terrace of houses built by his father for the Solomon Andrews Estate. With the exception of a brief period in Birmingham in 1927, and service with the RAF during the Second World War, Ifor lived at Arthog all his life.

The Higgon family hailed originally from Pembrokeshire. John, the father, was born in Mathry and while still a young man sought his first employment in Aberdare, with his brother, a stonemason. Later, John Higgon met Solomon Andrews, the Cardiff-based entrepreneur who, during the late 19th century, had established himself as a property developer and pioneer of public transport. When Andrews extended his business interests into mid and north Wales, John Higgon accompanied him and settled eventually in Arthog, where his practical skills were fully appreciated by the burgeoning company; by displaying good command of english and mathematics, he established himself as the foreman mason before being made the Arthog Estate manager.

Little is known of Gwladys, John Higgon's wife, but three children were raised at Arthog. Mattie became a teacher in Somerset, David qualified as a pharmacist and settled in Ilford, whilst Ifor remained at Arthog and, with the exception of the instances mentioned, lived in the same house all his life. Seemingly, all three youngsters were able and diligent but due possibly to some ill-health or family circumstances, Ifor appears to have been denied an opportunity to further his education beyond attendance at the local grammar school in Barmouth, located just a mile or so across the estuary from his home. This entailed a daily journey by train across the long viaduct which still spans the river at this point – surely, one of the most sublime school journeys imaginable. This was to be the extent of Ifor's formal education, although he appears to have been an accomplished scholar, revealing a particular aptitude for mathematics, science and practical subjects. Throughout his life, he continued to read widely, nurturing interests in astronomy, geology, horology, history and ornithology, particularly as applied to his immediate natural and industrial environment. He frequently noted unusual wildlife and bird activity in the area and his diaries also record exceptional weather conditions, such as:

'*Thursday 24 Feb. 1927. Splendid day.*

In evening at 7.0 pm saw zodiacal light in the form of a cone rising from the ocean in the west and extending half-way across the heavens at an acute angle of about 70° with horizon.'

Although of a friendly disposition, Ifor Higgon was essentially a retiring and private person, and he did not easily discuss personal aspects of his life. The sparse information now available to us has been gleaned from a run of small Cyclists' Diaries, measuring on average a mere 3ins by 2ins, which he maintained between 1927 and 1969; all have survived, with the exception of those for 1928 and 1936. Ifor mentioned them only a short time before he died – too late to allow any analysis of their content. The brief notes which follow are based on these small diaries.

THE EARLY YEARS

In addition to possessing practical skills and an enquiring mind, Higgon was physically active from his earliest days. He was passionately fond of cycling throughout his life and owned several cycles at various times, including two built by F.R. Grubb, his pride and joy being the special lightweight machine hand-built and tailor-made to his personal specification. When he took delivery of it on 17th January 1927 he noted:

'*Bicycle arrived from F.R. Grubb by 10.0 am train. Looks splendid, runs splendidly.*'

From this time, records of his monthly mileages were painstakingly compiled, together with detailed logs of his more lengthy journeys, noting times, road surfaces and weather conditions – much in the manner of train performance records which, as a 16-year old, he had also started to compile. Despite the later purchase of another Grubb cycle in March 1940 and a Dawes Galaxy in June 1974, his original machine received meticulous care and attention over the years and remained in constant use until, in May 1987, a simple note records:

'*70110 miles; bike dismantled, aged 60 years+*'

Cycling had occupied a special place in his affections and, even when well into his 80s, Ifor cycled regularly across the viaduct to collect his pension in Barmouth. The bicycle had proved an ideal adjunct for observing and photographing the Cambrian line.

When in his early 20s, he prepared two illustrated articles, supported by his own photographs, which were published in the *Railway Magazine* in June 1928 and August 1930. In common with many other enthusiasts, he also derived great pleasure from collecting artifacts and old railway documents, the latter not merely as possessions but because he sought to safeguard the information they contained; he displayed a keen sense of history. Most of his material has already been deposited at the National Museum of Wales. Old *Working Time Tables* and *Weekly Notices* appealed especially to him. Each division of the railway produced its own dedicated version of the latter, which were not intended for public use; they were difficult to acquire. As official documents they were normally destroyed as soon as they had expired, in order to eliminate the risk of confusion with each succeeding issue, for as their title indicates, a new notice emerged each week. The vast majority were destroyed as intended. Today, any surviving *Weekly Notices* are prized as valuable historic documents, for they chronicle the minutiae of the railway's day-to-day working and provide us with detailed information which was not recorded elsewhere. Ifor Higgon derived great satisfaction from tracking down and safeguarding such material.

His photographic collection, however, indicates he was more than a mere compiler of official matter. Surviving negatives reveal that roll-film was used quite extensively during the early and mid 1930s; thereafter, 2B photographic plates found favour, although the cameras used during those early years are unknown, until the switch to the 35mm format during the 1960s. Processing appears to have held little appeal for him – other than a small bakealite tank for developing 2B plates, he left nothing in the way of darkroom equipment. His output seems to have waxed and waned over the years, and he seems not have seen prints of all of his work until the late C.C. Green undertook the production of a series of postcard sized proofs for him, around the late 1950s.

In addition to creating his own images, Higgon collected early prints of the railway whenever he came across them, being one of the first as far as the Cambrian was concerned. Some were gifts, others were purchased from railway friends for a modest half-a-crown or five shillings (12^1/$_2$p or 25p today) – a pittance by today's reckoning but a respectable enough 'tip' in those days.

Together with his own photographs – commenced in 1924 – and assemblage of printed matter, his collection of archive prints contribute to his role as an observer, recorder and archivist. Furthermore, his punctilious lineside observation of train movements, particularly on busy summer Saturdays, present us with unique records of traffic at specific locations and dates.

In view of the foregoing, it may seem a bit churlish to record a few shortcomings but certain aspects of the railway scene were ignored by him when one might have assumed that they would have held greater appeal. Prominent amongst these was an almost complete disregard of station and signal box views, whilst certain locomotive classes also failed to attract his attention. The steam railmotors, introduced by the GWR soon after the 1923 Grouping, failed completely to inspire him to take a single photograph, although he had used the cars on a daily basis to and from the County School in Barmouth. Nor did he pay that much heed to their operation down the coast even though their territory extended at one time between Machynlleth, Criccieth and Dolgellau – unless they happened to fail and had to be replaced by more conventional (usually Cambrian) motive power. He paid little attention to them and, similarly, the GWR's 2-8-0 engines of the '28/38XX' and ROD '30XX' classes which operated between Ruabon and Barmouth Junction also failed to capture his imagination; he did not photograph them either, although he did at least note their numbers. He remains the primary (possibly the only) source of information concerning the operation of these engines over this route. Other visitors on freight duty between Ruabon and Barmouth Junction at that time were the 2-6-0 'Aberdare' Class. Over twenty different members of the class were noted by Ifor over more than a decade, yet they are represented in the Higgon photographic register by a solitary, rather prosaic, portrait of No. 2617 at Barmouth Junction, waiting to return to Ruabon with the last Up freight of the day, on 31st May 1930.

Again, although Higgon lived in a land of narrow gauge railways the majority, disappointingly, failed to command his attention. The exceptions were the Padarn and Penrhyn Quarry railways, which were virtually the only ones to generate any sustained interest. The mighty Ffestiniog, together with more local lines at Corris and Tal-y-llyn, failed to motivate him, this at a time when both the 2ft 3in gauge lines were operating passenger services; he managed only a handful of engine portraits up to 1930. Thereafter, he did not return to them, although the Corris continued to carry slate until 1948 and the Tal-y-llyn – like the Windmill Theatre – never closed. Of the quartet of photographs recorded on the Corris, Higgon's most important contribution was his portrayal of withdrawn No. 2 in store at Machynlleth in 1927 (see *Railway Through Talerddig*, Gomer Press, 1990, p70)

but he seems to have been totally unaware of the existence at that time of the equally fascinating hulk of erstwhile No. 1, which lay in the open at the end of a siding at Maespoeth. He ignored this location although he must have been aware of it, having cycled past on countless occasions.

Similarly, he showed no interest in photographing the Vale of Rheidol or the Welshpool & Llanfair and, despite being undoubtedly knowledgeable regarding the Fairbourne line – his immediate neighbour – he failed to leave a single photograph of these little trains either.

As some compensation for such omissions, it must be acknowledged that Ifor Higgon is believed to be the first person to compile detailed records of train timings over the Cambrian line. They date from around 1924 and although predictably few in number, feature an intriguing variety of locomotive classes. These range from Cambrian '94' Class 4-4-0s (Large Belpaire) to GWR 'Barnum' 2-4-0s, 'Duke' Class 4-4-0s and more modern locomotives such as the Collett 'Manors' and Riddles 'Standard' Class '4' 4-6-0s. Regrettably, Churchward's versatile 2-6-0s, the '43xx' Class – in many ways ideally suited to and well liked on the Cambrian – failed to feature in his notes. Some might well smile and query the merit of recording train times over a line where speeds were only modest at best and where gradients, frequent stops, severe speed restrictions and long single track sections suggested there was little here to attract the prominent train recorders of the day. Higgon, however, was content to note the often excellent results achieved by enginemen who operated comparatively small and under-powered locomotives in difficult circumstances.

Brother David appears to have shared the interest in railways during the early 1920s but there is no evidence to suggest that this was sustained, as he concentrated on his career as a pharmacist in Ilford. Meanwhile, in 1927, Ifor had embarked on a career in industrial chemistry with the Dunlop Company in Birmingham. Whilst on a preliminary visit to Fort Dunlop on 5th May 1927, he noted:

'No. 3802 4-4-0 'County Clare' at Salop, with the 8-wheeled tender from the 'Great Bear'.'

He commenced at Dunlop's on Monday 16th May and in an endeavour to 'settle in' to his new surroundings, continued his hobby whenever he could. On his first free Saturday afternoon, he took a train to Dunstall Park (fare 3s 4d) to:

'visit Wolverhampton old shed and Oxley sidings … 4171 4-4-0 Armstrong partly dismantled.'

His interests were not confined to the Great Western, for he occasionally visited New Street station, where on Friday 27th May, for example, he noted:

'L&YR loco (outs cyls) working ex Derby about 10.25pm.'

Previously, at around 10.10 p.m. on the evening of Monday 23rd May he had also noted:

'Turbo loco working ex Derby, and a new LMS 2-6-0 13xxx class.'

He soon realised the need for a bicycle and by the end of that week he had taken delivery of his 'lightweight' from Arthog (carriage 7s 11d), which was put to immediate use the following day when, on Sunday 29th May, he cycled to Derby, noting in his diary – with customary diligence:

'Went on Lightweight to Derby (Dep. 12.30: Arr 3.50pm; 39.5 miles)'

and on returning that evening he wrote:

'*Saw Litchfield Cathedral – very beautiful … country rich but rather monotonous*'.

The following day he claimed he was:

'*not tired but suffering from saddle-soreness.*'

Nonetheless, by the end of the week he had set off again, this time to cycle from Birmingham home to Arthog:

'*via Wellington, Salop* [sic], *Welshpool, Llanfair* [Careinion] *and Dinas* [Mawddwy]. *Dep. 7.0am, arrived home 6.30pm. For the last 85 miles, strong headwind against … had to fight for every foot of the way.*'

An achievement which speaks much of his fortitude.

On a more prosaic level, lesser beings occasionally caught his eye, including a Sentinel/Cammell steam locomotive shunting at Fort Dunlop sidings, relieving the regular LM&SR 0-4-0T No. 1516, on 5th July 1927. Then, the following day, 6th July, Higgon noted:

'*GWR 4-6-0 4-cyl No. 6000 … Design similar to Castle class.*'

Neither location nor livery were recorded by him, nor was there any reference to a name. Eric Mountford, in his *Swindon GWR Reminiscences* (Bradford Barton, 1982) claims to have been totally surprised, on 24th June 1927, by the sight of *King George V*, in works grey, emerging from 'A' Shop, whilst Alan Peck, in *The Great Western at Swindon Works* (OPC, 1983), records that No. 6000 had been photographed, in works grey on 16th June. The 'King' was thus virtually brand new when noted by Higgon in Birmingham, essentially being only days old and having been seen by comparatively few people. Yet the significance of his sighting appeared to have made no great impression on him.

His stay at Fort Dunlop, however, seems not to have been particularly enjoyable or rewarding. This might be attributed partly to disenchantment with the unchallenging nature of the work (he had previously noted '*Still plodding on with the work at Dunlop's*') in addition to indifferent health at this time and partly to:

'*rotten lodgings, rotten food, meals anyhow, any old time, any old thing.*'

The diaries of this era contain frequent references to heart or foot problems – '*Foot bad*' or '*Foot better*' being fairly typical comments over these years – yet Higgon had previously led an active life and in addition to cycling, had also played some football and cricket since leaving school. At this juncture, it is difficult to determine the precise nature of these complaints but it is evident that indifferent health beset him most of his life. In this instance, poor food and lodging and low spirits – combined possibly with a dash of job disappointment – caused the abandonment of his projected career with the Dunlop Company. He left Dunlop's on Friday 11th December 1927 and duly returned to Arthog where, under the *aegis* of his father as manager of the Solomon Andrews property, he found ready employment. His time was mainly spent repairing and maintaining various properties, where his versatility was invaluable but, occasionally, he also exercised freedom to diversify, as occurred in August 1935, when he played an official role in a traffic census.

Although light repairs and other building work continued to occupy him, the railway observations chronicled in his diaries during this period seemed to increase. These possibly reflected the heavy summer passenger traffic from Birmingham and Paddington to Cardigan Bay, as the country recovered slowly from the effects of economic depression. These services, in addition to the Cambrian's well established links with the Manchester area,

ensured that summer weekends were particularly busy periods. There were instances, right up to the outbreak of war in 1939, of special excursion trains diagrammed to run throughout the night on Fridays, due to the lack of clear paths over the single line Cambrian on Saturdays. Furthermore, several of the through services perpetuated the practice of earlier years and ran in more than one portion (some examples are noted in *Talerddig in Great Western Days*, Gomer Press, 1999, pp91-92).

It was during this pre-war period that Higgon extended his sphere of interest to include some of the minor by-ways which hitherto had avoided his gaze. Those situated along the Welsh Marches were accessible by cycle, provided an early morning start was made from Arthog. As this entailed departure around 03.30, the operation was usually confined to the months of May or June, to take the fullest advantage of longer daylight hours. Thus the Shropshire & Montgomeryshire Railway was visited in June 1930, when a few photographs of (largely) derelict rolling stock were taken. The only general view was a single photograph of Kinnerley shed; panoramic station views did not appeal to him and generally do not feature in his work. The Bishop's Castle Railway, visited in June 1932, was another which drew his attention during this period but where he again confined himself to views of stationary stock and managed to return without capturing a single image of a typical service train.

THE SECOND WORLD WAR

The onset of the Second World War saw Higgon serving in the Home Guard, despite continued complaints of indifferent health. However, by 27th July 1940, he had been medically examined under the provisions of the National Registration Act and passed Grade 1. 'Call-up' was then expected to follow within four or five weeks but nothing occurred until October 1940, when, still a civilian, he was called to Euston House for interview with the RAF London AV Board (sic). He initially entertained thoughts of serving in the RAF as a pilot or navigator but these ambitions were not fulfilled, possibly due to his age and general medical condition.

His journey to London, for the interview, started from Barmouth Junction behind 2-6-0 No. 6348 on the 10.25am to Ruabon. There he continued behind No. 2989 *Talisman* to Wolverhampton, where an unidentified 'King' worked the train forward to arrive at Paddington by 6.30pm. This occurred at the height of the blitz and Higgon was compelled to spend that night, with countless others, attempting to snatch what sleep he could in a cold and crowded waiting room. After his interview the following day, that night was spent at the Gordon Hospital, Victoria, as air-raids raged all night, from around 7.00pm to 7.00am. The following morning he again visited Euston House, before returning to Paddington for the 2.10pm to Birkenhead, behind another unidentified 'King' in charge of a packed fifteen coach train. Given the circumstances, an additional hour and a half was required to reach Birmingham. Matters did not improve as Arthog was not reached until 11.30pm.

During this period, John Higgon's health was failing and Ifor had to undertake the role of Estate Manager. As his 'call-up' became imminent, the company found difficulty in securing a suitably versatile replacement for him. At this time, skilled tradesmen in the area were being attracted *en masse* to the construction of the new military establishments along the coast – the RAF at Llanbedr, Commando bases at Aberdyfi, Arthog and Barmouth,

A classic Cambrian scene of the early 1950s on Talerddig Bank, as 'Earl' Class No. 9001 assists Class '43xx' 2-6-0 No. 6321 of Tyseley shed with the 2.20pm train from Aberystwyth to Birmingham on 1st August 1953. The 'Earls' were to an extent rebuilds, using the frames of withdrawn 'Bulldogs' and the cabs of scrapped 'Dukes', and were constructed in two batches between 1936 and 1939. Originally No. 3201 *St. Michael*, the 4-4-0 lost its plates within a fortnight of being built in May 1936 and then ran nameless for another two weeks, before being renamed *Earl of Dunraven*. This was again fairly short-lived, however, the class (with the exception of *Tre Pol and Pen*) all losing their names in 1937. Renumbering in to the '90xx' series took place in 1946 and the engine was withdrawn just nine months after this picture was taken, in April 1954

the Royal Marines camp at Llwyngwril but, particularly, the large Royal Artillery bases at Tywyn and Tonfanau; there was an abundance of work for skilled tradesmen in the area.

Ifor was relieved of this problem by reporting to Padgate on 10th April 1940, where his stay was brief as he was promptly transferred, in fairly rapid succession, to Bournemouth, Yatesbury, Henbury, St. Mawgan and Trevone. The Yatesbury posting was significant, as it was then one of the major radar training establishments in the UK. In that distant pre-calculator, pre-computer era, the mathematically competent were readily welcomed into branches of the services which were becoming increasingly dependent on technology. Higgon's ability was noted and whilst based at Trevone, he was called to a further interview, in July 1941, at Adastral House, in London. Eventually, this led to a posting to Rodel Park, a radar station on the remote southernmost tip of the Isle of Harris, in the Outer Hebrides. Here he was destined to be stationed for the remainder of his service career. Whilst this might appear to the less initiated to have been something of a backwater, it was in fact a good location to monitor the busy Atlantic traffic to and from America.

During this period, photography played no part in his life, as practical difficulties and restrictions affected the hobby during the war years; furthermore, railways, docks and industrial locations were extremely sensitive subjects – many carried positive prohibitions – whilst the availability of film photographic paper and chemicals was extremely limited. Higgon's railway interest was therefore confined to notes made during his essential rail journeys, usually when he was transferred between bases or went on leave. Despite their sketchy nature, they now make interesting reading, particularly when they entailed travel over lines 'foreign' to the Great Western; journeys across LM&SR or SR territory were noted with interest. Most of his sparse war-time observations along the Cambrian have been incorporated previously in the RC&TS's *Locomotives of the Great Western Railway* series or the writer's own *Talerddig in Great Western Days*. The only Cambrian account included here features the brief note made when returning to Wilmslow on Friday 7th January 1944, for his discharge from the RAF.

He had joined the 12.35pm train from Aberystwyth at Dovey Junction. This Whitchurch-bound service was then an 'all-stations' stopping train as far as Welshpool – it even stopped at Commins Coch, which was never popular with the crews of Up services. Throughout his life, Ifor described the composition of passenger trains (which in his early days often consisted of mixed 8, 6, or 4-wheeled stock) in the manner much favoured pre-war, when coaches were usually referred to according to the number of wheels, hence '8s, 6s or 4s', as the case might be. That day, No. 7819 *Hinton Manor* worked its load of '9.8s' (nine bogies) forward from Machynlleth without assistance, a common enough occurrence during the 1940s when 'Manors' frequently took nine coaches single-handedly over Talerddig (or occasionally ten if the footplate crews felt the state of the engine, and the coal, were adequate). Higgon noted No. 7819's performance simply:

'*Mach.* Dt. 1.28.30s .... [T/T 1.29.00]
Tal. arr. 2.3.15s .... [T/T 2.3.00]
net 32 mins 35s. Minimum 18 m.p.h.'

A creditable performance by a 'Manor' during war-time conditions.

Two examples of journeys outside Wales feature in the diaries;

the first outlines a July 1941 journey from Trevone via Padstow to Paddington and the subsequent return trip, which was via the Southern from Waterloo. For this interview, at Adastral House, Higgon was able to stay overnight with brother David in Ilford. The account is presented as written and calls for little additional comment other than to indicate that No. 6913 *Levens Hall* was then a new engine, having emerged from Swindon barely four months previously; it was also one of the last of the original 'Halls' to carry its name when built. No's 6916 - 6970, constructed later during the war, remained nameless until the 1946-48 period:

'*25 Fri. Fine hot day. leave Padstow SR 8.2pm to Bodmin. 3M. Walk to Bodmin Rd. but had lift. Then GWR via Plymouth to Padd. Saw foll. 4550, 5526, 5915 PZ, 5140, Up gds 4090. Went on relief to 10.53 Up 6913 4-6-0 9.8s to Plymouth then via Direct line.*

26 Sat. Padd arr. 6.15am 'King' from Plymouth. To Adastral House 9.30am - 3.0pm, then to Dei [David]. Wet day. Interview re. A1, with F/O Daniels Room 567. Got on O.K.

27 Sun. Nice afternoon. Went with Dei to Hainault Golf Course. Dei had 18 rounds [sic]. Nice open breezy course on wooded uplands. Raid by Jerry, night 2 - 4 am passing over.

28 Mon. Leave Dei 9.0am Barking ungd to Monument. Change & then Bank - Waterloo. Dt 11am. 4-6-0 Lord Nelson class 15.8s via Woking, Salisbury. Saw here 2829, 26xx, 2955. Salisbury 12.40 - 1.0pm. From Sal. 4-6-0 449 Sir Torre 9.Bs. Yeovil, Sidmouth Jct. Exeter. From EXE 2x 4-4-0s 9.8s EXE GWR 3590, 2-4-0T, 5543, 4829. From Yeoford Jct. 2-6-0 1860, 9.8s to Padstow worked very hard. Padstow 6.40pm. Walk to Trevone. SRy engines Nelson & King Arthur very speedy and silent. Nice working. 36 hrs off. Fresh SW showers.'

A journey across Scotland between 11th and 14th May 1942, undertaken when he was already established at Rodel Park, provides an interesting contrast. The purpose of the trip is not mentioned but may have been a hospital visit.

'*11 Mon. On 3 pm bus to Stornaway. Fine day. Pictures evening, 'William Penn'.*

12 Tue. Leave on 'Loch Ness' 4.30am Calm xing.

*Kyle arr. 10.30am. Went up to Church of Scotland canteen for breakfast. Kyle dt. 11.30am. 14*** Clan Cameron. 8.8s.*

[At] Kyle 14412 Ben Avon, 17951, 14764 Clan Munro.

Inverness arr. 3.40pm. 5465/5166/5160; 4.15pm. 5173 & 5365; 2358 SR; 14692 4-6-0 Darnaway Castle; 15001 0-4-2T; 17821/2 2-6-0s 5012; 15226 0-4-4T; 16341; 17954; 5164; YMCA night.

13 Wed. To Bunchrew 7.15 transport. To Inverness 11.45am.

14768 Clan Mackenzie 8.8s; Inverness 5122; 5456; 5018; 15001; 14415 Ben Bhach Ard; ex Dingwall 14400 Ben More ass. in front. Dn train Auchterneed 17954, 14764, 14400 to Achnashellach; Kyle arr. 5.0pm. Dt. on boat 5.50pm. Storn 12.20am.

emb. 70W night. [70W = RAF HQ Stornaway].

14 Thurs. Back on 9.30 am. bus. nice day.'

Life at Rodel Park cannot always have been easy, especially during winter months, but Higgon appears to have adapted well and mostly enjoyed the experience. He particularly appreciated the welcome of local folk and much enjoyed the rugged beauty of the location, being once moved to attempt a series of 'thumb-nail' sketches of the island panorama. There were instances when the monotony of camp life was relieved when he was entertained by some of the crofters and taken occasionally on a fishing trip, or invited for a most welcome taste of home cooking. Such kindness was easily reciprocated by repairs to clocks and radios. As radar was being developed and constantly improved, the operators were subjected to a succession of courses for up-grading their knowledge and skills; there were regular tests and examinations, although these held no fear for him for he coped well with them. In addition to any natural aptitude, he studied conscientiously, and consistently scored high marks which usually placed him at the head of the group. This ensured his promotion during 1943, first to Corporal then Sergeant, when he was frequently in charge at Rodel Park.

Ill-health, however, continued to accompany him throughout his service career. During his time at Rodel he was increasingly troubled by kidney problems, being hospitalised for periods at Stornaway, Inverness and Wilmslow, which eventually led to his discharge on medical grounds. He left Rodel on 28th December 1943 on ten days sick leave, before reporting to the hospital at Wilmslow for further tests and X-rays, resulting finally in his discharge on 31st January 1944.

ARTHOG AGAIN

When Ifor returned to Arthog, he was quickly welcomed to his former employment on the Andrews Estate. In later years, he supplemented his earnings when he served as a postman in the locality, whilst his interest in the railway continued seamlessly. Initially, much remained as before the war, the early post-war years proving to be the final period when the railways held sway, prior to the private motor-car really beginning to dominate UK transport. Summer passenger traffic had reverted quickly to the rail-orientated pre-war pattern. Furthermore, the military bases along the coast remained active, prompted by various crises – the 'Cold War', the Korean conflict, the Suez Crisis and 'Z' training – this latter aimed at mobilisation and re-training of the reserve forces. Although traffic may not perhaps have been quite as intense as during the war, it was, nonetheless, sufficient to promote a succession of double-headed passenger trains over the summits of Garneddwen and Talerddig, whilst the three daily through goods workings from Machynlleth were all banked regularly over the latter incline, well into the 1950s.

Comparatively few photographs were taken by Ifor during this period. Just eight were taken in 1939, whilst in 1940, only six exposures were made (five of these on the Shropshire & Montgomeryshire Railway). No further photographs were taken during the war period and Higgon revealed no interest in photography on discharge from the RAF in 1944; only two feature in his register for 1945. Half a dozen were recorded in 1946 and succeeding years generated a mere handful; during the whole of 1951, only one railway photograph was taken. In comparison, 1952 witnessed a veritable explosion of photographs, when no fewer than seventeen exposures were made. Interestingly, this coincides with marginal improvements in the availability of photograhic materials and also, the acquisition of a motor-cycle which notably increased accessability and stimulated interest. For example, twelve of these images were taken on former Mid-Wales railway territory, around St. Harmon and Pantydwr, which were then brought within easier reach. From this period, such locations began to feature more frequently in his photographic register, although all were within Wales. There seems to have been no inclination to venture beyond the old

pre-war parameters, nor, it seems, was Higgon ever tempted to re-visit any of his war-time haunts. Padstow and Inverness commend themselves as obvious candidates, for both locations seem to have appealed to him during the early 1940s; picture albums of former LM&SR lines in the Highlands, for example, were prominent in his library.

Yet, although there was a reduction in the number of railway photographs taken between 1939-1952, there was no lessening of railway interest and Ifor's observation of railway operation was undiminished. Notes of locomotive movements continued to feature prominently in the small Cyclists' Diaries, with details being expanded slightly as they were re-written in notebooks during long winter evenings or weekends. Similarly, the observation and timing of locomotive performances continued to interest him, particularly as some of the logs now featured the new post-war locomotive types. He had always been attracted to the larger locomotives ranging the Cambrian, from the indigenous 4-4-0s and 'Dukes' of earlier days, to the later 'Manors' and British 'Standard' Class '75xxx's. These served to generate some interest amongst a few later enthusiasts but Ifor Higgon's meticulous notes, recorded from the mid-1920s, provide a valuable insight into steam operation on the Cambrian. Official railway paperwork and time tables maintained their fascination for him and he continued to safeguard the few *Special Notices* which came his way.

From the 1950s through to 1964 was a particularly productive period photographically, with 1960 being the peak year when over eighty images were made. Thereafter, production in 1965 and 1966 was much reduced and by the following year only four exposures were made. His most adventurous move during the period of decline of steam on BR would appear to have been his participation in a continental rail tour, possibly with the RC&TS, although this is unconfirmed. By this time he was using a 35mm Practika camera but, as previously, he relied on standard commercial processing. If notes and dates of this tour were originally recorded (and it is difficult to imagine that they were not) they have not survived and many of the proof prints which remain lack contrast and appeal.

The demise of steam along the Cambrian in 1967, however, caused Ifor Higgon to lay his camera aside. Only rare exceptions, such as the passage of LM&SR 'Pacific' No. 6203 *Princess Margaret Rose* from Butlins Holiday Camp at Pwllheli to Shrewsbury via Machynlleth in 1975, and a few occasions in 1987 when No's 7819 and 75069 brought steam back to the area, tempted him to take his camera again to the Friog and Morfa Mawddach. He was not to experience the photographic advances of the digital revolution, although the new technology, particularly the ease of processing, might well have appealed to him. However, he was content, for he had experienced some glorious Cambrian and Great Western years when the engines, even the later BR 'Standards' and small Ivatts, were of the same fraternity – they all emitted steam. Diesels held no attraction for him.

But what might he have made of Stanier's 'Black Fives' running 'down the coast'? Given the opportunity, he would surely have taken a camera again on to the Friog? As it transpired, there was little to interest him, other than photographing the havoc wrought by the Teredo worm on Barmouth viaduct in 1981-2.

Ifor Higgon passed away on 30th December 1996.

1
HIGGON'S SQUARE MILE
AROUND BARMOUTH JUNCTION

An undated photograph of a line inspection working behind GWR 'Stella' Class 2-4-0 No. 3503, probably in the later 1920s. New in September 1892, the engine was withdrawn in July 1929. When the GWR leased the Bristol & Exeter Railway in 1876, a batch of First/Second Composite standard gauge coaches were in the course of delivery. By 1892, eight of them had been rebuilt into inspection coaches on longer underframes with verandah ends. This example had been fitted with flare lamps on the roof for tunnel inspections and carried additional side lamps. These inspection coaches had long lives, the first being withdrawn in 1936 and the last not until 1959.

Ex-Cambrian Railways No. 67, photographed at Barmouth Junction as GWR No. 1100 on 16th February 1928, with a returning officer's inspection saloon, *en route* to Oswestry. Locomotive and tender were painted plain GWR green. This class of handsome 4-4-0s was built for the Cambrian by Sharp, Stewart & Co., twenty being constructed between 1893 and 1898. Two more added, No's 19 and 11 in 1901 and 1904 respectively, which held the honour of being the only locomotives built by the Cambrian at their Oswestry Works. No. 67 was new in May 1893 and withdrawn in July 1930. The coach was one of a pair of Engineer's Saloons built in 1876. Initially numbered in the First Class coaches series, then as Saloon No. 9220 in 1908 (Diagram G29), this one was finally renumbered in 1923 as No. 80943 in the goods stock series (coaching stock diagram Q7) and was withdrawn in January 1936. The officials travelled in the end furthest from the camera, where there were end windows to give a good view of the line.

Sharp, Stewart-built, ex-Cambrian Railways No. 48, as GWR No. 908, along with '517' Class 0-4-2T No. 1155, double-head the mid-day 'Up' goods from Barmouth Junction on 27th August 1931. No. 1155, which had probably spent two weeks or so operating the Penmaenpool auto service to Barmouth, was returning to Machynlleth, its parent shed, for periodic routine maintenance and was assisting the train engine on the way. Both locomotives were nearing the end of long, sixty year-plus careers, the 0-6-0 having been built in 1873 and the 0-4-2T two years later; they were withdrawn in December 1938 and February 1936 respectively. The private owner wagon next to the tank engine was some distance from its home patch, belonging to the Bestwood Coal & Iron Co. of Nottingham and possibly numbered 333. The company became part of BA Collieries Ltd in 1936. Behind it is an iron-bodied 'Iron Mink' van.

An impressive pairing of two 'Dean Goods', No's 2468 and 2572, double-heading the seven-coach 12.20 Up passenger train from Barmouth to Machynlleth away from Barmouth Junction on 19th September 1936. These sturdy 0-6-0s were one of William Dean's most successful designs, the class eventually totalling 260 members built between 1883 and 1899. Sixty-two of the class saw service with the Railway Operating Department (ROD) in France and also Salonika during the First World War but No's 2468 and 2572 were not amongst those called up. Over a hundred 'Dean Goods' were then requisitioned during the Second World War but, again, the two engines seen here avoided that fate too. Most that were called up either did not come back from overseas or were returned as unfit for further use and scrapped. New in 1896, No. 2468 was withdrawn in early 1953, whilst No. 2572's working life was slightly shorter, from 1898 to 1952.

With the intended eventual replacement motive power, the 'Manor' Class 4-6-0s, still on the drawing board, Swindon's 'quick-fix' for the Cambrian line's shortage of adequate locomotives at this time was to rapidly produce a series of moderately costed engines by marrying the more robust frames of withdrawn 'Duke' Class engines. Here, No. 3214, barely two months 'old' and sporting an immaculate green livery, was being turned at Barmouth Junction whilst working a Ministry of Transport Special Train, around the coast from Aberystwyth to Ruabon, on 3rd November 1937.

Following on from the previous picture, very little is known of the train No. 3214 is seen hauling away from the junction later that day, no documentation regarding it having yet been discovered. The first vehicle is believed to be Saloon No. 9004 (or possibly No. 9005). At that time, both these prestigious VIP carriages were used only by the General Manager or the highest-ranking officers of the GWR. Nothing is known of its passengers nor duty on this occasion, nothing has emerged of their point of origin or final destination nor indeed, the route taken to reach Aberystwyth in the first instance. At the time of the picture, an uneasy peace existed throughout Europe, as war had not yet been declared although, significantly, it was the topic uppermost in everyone's mind. Could it have been that the occupants of No. 9004 were reviewing local options and arrangements for the forthcoming conflict, which looked increasingly imminent? It may perhaps only be a coincidence but, from this time, the coast of Cardigan Bay was to become a frenzy of building activity as military camps and airfields were rapidly constructed, the area being speedily transformed into a vast training ground. If this is indeed what these pictures show, then their full significance is only now coming to light.

Working practices changed very little over the years. Replicating the format of the 1931 working, No. 3265 *Tre Pol and Pen* leads 2-6-2T No. 4549 with a sizeable train of largely empty wagons forming the mid-day goods from the coast to Machynlleth on 20th August 1947.

'Bulldog' Class 4-4-0 No. 3450 *Peacock* in the process of turning on the triangle at Barmouth Junction, having worked the 7.00am Wrexham to Barmouth passenger train on 11th October 1935, a regular working for this Croes Newydd-based locomotive at this time. The 'Bulldog' 4-4-0s were another of Dean's successful designs, with 121 built new and a further twenty rebuilt from 'Duke' Class engines, all between 1899 and 1906. In 1909-10, fifteen more were built with strengthened outside frames and these were numbered into a separate sub-class, the 'Birds', with No. 3450 *Peacock* being one of this final batch, constructed in December 1909. The engine enjoyed a forty-year career, being withdrawn early into the British Railways era in December 1949. On a sunny autumn day, the enginemen adopt a relaxed pose for the photographer's portrait of their handsome steed.

During early September 1954, 0-4-2T No. 1465 suffered a major failure whilst working the Dolgelley-Barmouth auto service at Arthog, when the spokes of one of its trailing wheels fractured. Fortunately, a more serious incident did not result and No. 1465 was removed temporarily to Garth Siding at Arthog, where it was photographed by Ifor on 10th September 1954. An initial replacement service was provided by a Crossville bus, whilst the engine was eventually repaired and returned to service.

Another failure the following year saw a Western Region Class '22xx' 0-6-0 replaced at Rhyl by 1886-built, ex-Midland/LM&SR Johnson Class '2P' 4-4-0 No. 40377, which was hurriedly pressed into service to work the return leg of a Western Region 'Land Cruise' train back to Pwllheli, on 30th June 1955. It was recorded heading north away from Barmouth Junction. No. 40377 was near the end of a very long life; built at Derby in December 1886 and on its final allocation, to Llandudno Junction shed, it was to be withdrawn just two months after Ifor took the picture.

A view from just below road level at the highest point of the Friog incline, taken circa 1925, sometime before the landslip occurred and therefore, before the cliff face was fully strengthened

2
ALONG THE COAST

RIGHT: 'Duke' Class 4-4-0s were numerous in the area following the Grouping. No. 3277 *Isle of Tresco* was a typical example, its name reflecting the original purpose of the class, built in the late 1890s for working expresses over the steep banks of Devon and Cornwall. Here, it leaves the junction with the 1.35pm for Pwllheli, on 1st May 1932.

BELOW: On shed at Porthmadog, No's 4575 and 4555 await their next turn of duty on 3rd April 1953. Note that No. 4555 has the original style of straight top tanks fitted to the '45xx' class, whilst No. 4575 was the first of these small 2-6-2Ts to be equipped with slope fronted, larger capacity water tanks when built in 1927. No. 4555 survived to be preserved and today has a home on the Dartmouth Steam Railway.

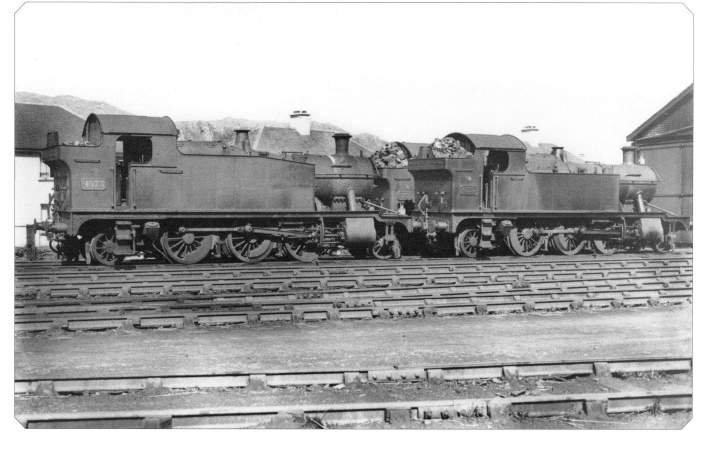

Light engine workings down the coast were not particularly numerous but No. 3265 *Tre Pol and Pen* was recorded climbing the Friog *en route* to Machynlleth and eventually Oswestry on 3rd August 1946. 'Duke' Class No. 3271 *Tre Pol and Pen* was new in July 1896, becoming No. 3265 in the GWR's December 1912 renumbering programme. Withdrawn in December 1929 and then dismantled, some parts of the locomotive were married to a spare 'Duke' boiler and a set of 'Bulldog' frames to produce the prototype of the 'Dukedogs'. This particular engine retained its 3ft 2ins diameter bogie wheels, however, and thus differed slightly from the rest of the class. In this form No. 3265 survived until withdrawn on 10th December 1949.

'Mogul' No. 5319 and 'Dukedog' Class 4-4-0 No. 9004, both of Croes Newydd shed (coded CNYD in GWR days and then 84J under BR) enter Barmouth Junction with a return holiday express, the 6.05pm Barmouth to Small Heath, on 30th July 1957.

On 30th May 1964, now preserved No. 7812 *Erlestoke Manor* was seen on brakedown crane duty at Barmouth Junction.

On 6th September 1958, No. 6371 of Machynlleth (89C) shed was photographed working the down CCE as it departed from the junction and made its way towards the long viaduct across the estuary. New in May 1921 and one of thirty-five of these highly versatile engines built for the GWR by Robert Stephenson & Co. in 1921-22, it had been a resident of Machynlleth shed since September 1951 but was to be transferred down to Exeter just eleven weeks after this picture was taken. Its stay there was short, however, for two months later it arrived back at Machynlleth, which was to be its home for the final twenty months of its working life, withdrawal taking place in September 1960. The three leading carriages of the train are in the BR version of the chocolate and cream livery, the first of which displays the BR coaching stock roundel on its side.

The Talyllyn Railway generated some special traffic, including a railtour run every year to carry members to their AGM. The first operated in 1953 and the special working is here epitomised by that run for the 1958 meeting on 27th September, with 'Dukedog' No. 9018 leading classmate No. 9004 along a stretch of track known as the 'deviation'. Colloquially referred to by Machynlleth crews as the 'Doveyation', this had been constructed when it was found impossible to bridge the estuary at Aberdyfi, as originally planned in the 1860s. On the footplate of No. 9018 on this occasion were engineman Len Edwards and fireman A.B. Jones of Machynlleth shed. Incidentally, the special was hauled from Paddington to Shrewsbury by ex-LM&SR 'Compound' 4-4-0 No. 41123, of Gloucester Barnwood shed; was this the first and possibly only visit of one of these engines to the erstwhile GWR's London terminus?

The Pwllheli portion of the Down Cambrian Coast Express, composed of seven coaches, is seen here on 20th June 1959 shortly after leaving Llanbedr & Pensarn station. Hauled by No. 7806 *Cockington Manor*, these lightweight 4-6-0s were built to work some of the heavier, longer distance trains on 'Blue' routes such as the Cambrian main line, in place of the '43xx' Class 2-6-0s. The first twenty, built just before the war in 1938-39, in fact incorporated the wheels and motion of withdrawn 'Moguls', such was the similarity of the breed. Representing the final piece in the jigsaw of GWR 4-6-0s for all purposes, they were such a success that a further ten were built in 1950 under British Railways. Although spread over the GWR system, they created a stir in 1943 when they became the first 4-6-0s to work over the Cambrian and have since become synonymous with it. New in March 1938, No. 7806 was withdrawn from Wolverhampton Oxley shed in November 1964.

Although the 4-4-0s were somewhat lighter on their feet than was ideal, they frequently undertook freight duties, as illustrated here by No. 9014 which was photographed hauling the 2.00pm Porthmadog-Machynlleth freight on Llangelynin Bank on 14th September 1959. When built in August 1937, as No. 3214, the engine was also allotted the name *Earl Waldegrave* but the nameplates were never carried. Apparently, the Earls whose names were chosen for these little engines were less than impressed with such unprepossessing machines, hence the decision to discontinue naming them and the removal of the plates from those already named, in summer 1937. The *Earl Waldegrave* plates were subsequently bestowed on 'Castle' Class 4-6-0 No. 5057 instead.

No. 9017 pilots BR 'Standard' Class '2' No. 78007 up Wern Bank with the 11.10am Paddington-Pwllheli (via Ruabon) on 25th June 1960. New in March 1953, the 2-6-0 was one of the members of the class to be painted in BR's passenger green livery. Its first allocation was to Oswestry shed but it was around two thirds of the way through a ten year stint stationed at Machynlleth at the date of this photograph. Withdrawal took place in May 1967, from Bolton shed. No. 9017 meanwhile, was another of the 'Dukedogs' allocated a name that was never carried, its intended *Earl of Berkeley* plates instead going to 'Castle' No. 5060, whilst its original No. 3217 numberplates were given to a Collett '22xx' 0-6-0 in 1946. The 'Dukedog' was bought by the Bluebell Railway a couple of years after withdrawal in 1960. In a hugely ironic twist, following the withdrawal of No. 5060 in 1962, it was finally named and was also re-united with its old numberplates in 1965 after No. 3217 was withdrawn.

The course of the railway through the Dyfi Valley was gently surveyed and Up trains approach Cemmes Road along a straight stretch of track much favoured photographically by Ifor Higgon, with the following three views, all taken in 1937, also at this location. Here, the 9:17am train from Barmouth to Paddington, hauled by 'Dukedog' 4-4-0 No. 3204 carrying train reporting No. 251, was piloted by GWR No. 884 on 21st August. The 0-6-0 was an ex-Cambrian Railways engine, their 'Large Goods' or '73' Class No. 87, built by Neilson, Reid & Co. in January 1899, which was providing assistance as far as Talerddig on this occasion. Fitted with a superheated boiler at Oswestry Works in 1931, it was the final member of the class of ten engines to remain in service, not quite making its way through the whole of the GWR era following withdrawal in August 1947. However, its service had been intended to end some time before this, as it was originlly withdrawn in 1939, along with No's 876 and 885, but all three were then quickly reinstated following the outbreak of war. No. 3204, meanwhile, was still relatively new when seen here, having been constructed in August 1936 from the frames of 'Bulldog' No. 3439 and parts from 'Earl' No. 3271. Originally named *Earl of Dartmouth*, the nameplates having been removed a few weeks before the photograph was taken, it was renumbered in to the '90xx' Series in July 1946 and lasted in service until June 1960. A little confusingly, Cemmes Road station served the village of Cemmaes Road, which is now called Glantwymyn.

3
MAIN LINE
1937-1962

RIGHT: The same location served for this unusual aspect of No. 3212 later that same morning, with the Down 8.20am local service from Oswestry to Aberystwyth. Built in May 1937, this was another of the 'Dukedogs' that was named but in this instance its *Earl of Eldon* plates were only carried for a very short time, as all of the 'Dukedogs' had lost their names by 1st July that year.

BELOW: Un-named 'Duke' Class No. 3289 piloting No. 3264 *Trevithick* with the 10.00am Up Cambrian Coast Express, carrying train reporting No. 250, had lost its *St. Austell* nameplates in July 1930, a decision taken by the Traffic Department after passengers complained that they were mistaking certain engine names for destinations!

ABOVE: Twelve years later, on 6th August 1949, Higgon re-visited Cemmes Road to record a similar but contemporary version of the scene, as 4-4-0 No. 9026 piloted No. 7802 *Bradley Manor* with a load of twelve bogie vehicles forming the Up CCE.

BELOW: Another 4-4-0/4-6-0 combination was captured on 20th September 1958, climbing Breidden Bank, east of Buttington. No. 7828 *Odney Manor* was being assisted by No 9018 from Machynlleth through to Shrewsbury, with another twelve coach CCE.

The position of the A470 road bridge over the railway at Carno proved to be another of Higgons's favoured locations, where he recorded former Lancashire & Yorkshire 2-4-2T No. 50781 piloting 4-4-0 No. 9021 on Talyllyn Railway Special train of 28th September 1957. The train was making its way from the sunshine of the upper Severn Valley towards the rain of Talerddig and the gloom of a damp reception further west. The first two coaches are again Collett large window 'Sunshine' stock.

The early afternoon Up freight from Machynlleth was traditionally referred to as the '2 o'clock goods', although, over the years, its time varied from around 1.50pm to 2.10pm. It was usually handled by '90' Class 4-4-0s or Collett '22xx' 0-6-0s, which almost invariably in those days required a banker, as here on 21st December 1957, when No. 3207 was receiving assistance from No. 5570, the longest serving 'Prairie' at Machynlleth.

No. 7801 *Anthony Manor* lifts the seven mixed-liveried coaches of the 12.40pm service from Aberystwyth to Whitchurch over Bell's Bridge, Talerddig, with no difficulty on 28th March 1959. The three two-tone coaches may well be in the short-lived carmine and cream ('blood & custard') livery of the 1950s, which looked very attractive but did not wear well in traffic, rather than the chocolate and cream paint scheme reintroduced by the Western Region in 1956. The leading coach is a Hawksworth design, with domed ends to the roof and almost flat sides. Allocated to Oswestry shed at the date of this view, January 1938-built No. 7801 was transferred to Shrewsbury in February 1963 and withdrawn from there in July 1965.

When the Western Region started building additional 'Manors' from 1950, the first three went to Oswestry, where their immediate deployment led to an instant reduction in banking duties. The difference the class made is best illustrated by comparing this view of No. 7819 *Hinton Manor*, working its way up the Dyfi Valley with the 1.45pm Machynlleth-Oswestry goods, on 11th September 1959, with that of the Collett 0-6-0 on the previous page, which required assistance with a similar length train. Note that the seventh wagon is a goods brake van. It appears that this working was regularly formed by combining two separate goods trains, as also shown on the previous page.

No. 7802 *Bradley Manor* glides smoothly down the bank from Talerddig, at the head of an immaculate set of coaches forming the Down Cambrian Coast Express on Saturday 3rd October 1959. First run under the CCE title in 1927, the train was re-introduced after the war running on Saturdays only. By 1957, BR had increased this to every day except Sundays. The normal weekday set comprised seven coaches including the Restaurant Car but, if for any reason the set had to be strengthened, as occurred occasionally, it ran the risk of attracting coaching stock of a different livery. Here, however, the photographer was fortunate and was able to leave us with this fine reminder of past glories, all eight coaches being in WR chocolate and cream. Note that the first two and last two coaches were carrying the circular BR coaching stock emblem, whilst the view also demonstrates that BR coaches (and Hawksworth ones) carried their destination boards just below the gutter at this period. Collett and earlier GWR coaches carried them on their roofs.

The 'Saturdays Only' 11.00am train from Ruabon to Pwllheli, hauled by 'Dean Goods' 0-6-0 No. 2468, had reached Drws-y-nant when Ifor Higgon photographed it on 11th September 1937. He positioned himself at the end of the loading bay immediately to the west of the platforms, to capture the fireman as he leant out to pick up the single line tablet from the Webb Thompson instrument, for the next section to Bontnewydd. This is our second encounter with No. 2468, which was clearly a regular on the route in the 1930s and had been allocated to Portmadoc shed since 1934. Note the pile of fence posts awaiting erection in the foreground. The leading coach in the train is a Collett all-Third with flush fitting windows, as introduced in 1929, next is a Brake Composite and the final vehicle is another all-Third. The brackets on the roofs for the destination boards show up well.

4
RUABON TO BARMOUTH
AND BALA TO BLAENAU FESTINIOG

RIGHT: The 12.10pm Barmouth to Manchester 'through train' leaves Bontnewydd behind Class '43xx' No. 5303, piloted by 'Bulldog' No. 3358 *Tremayne*, on 31st August 1935. Note the destination roofboards on the coaches and the presence of some clearestory roofed stock.

BELOW: Another of the versatile GWR 'Moguls', No. 5399, makes easy progress with the lightly laden 2.35pm Barmouth to Chester service, on Garneddwen Bank on 15th June 1957. This Chester West-based locomotive had been fitted with outside steam pipes just four months prior to the picture being taken. The leading van is a Southern Railway design Passenger Brake, known as a 'Van C' on the SR. It was quite a way from home. The carriages are a pair of Collett 'high waist' Thirds (now Seconds) and a Collett large window coach, possibly a Composite.

Another 4-4-0/2-6-0 combination double-head the 11.20am Pwllheli to Paddington train through Drws-y-Nant station on 6th September 1956. 'Dukedog' No. 9013 and 'Mogul' No. 6311 are gathering themselves to attack Garneddwen Bank, although the driver of the pilot engine has noticed Ifor and is leaning out of his cab to have his picture taken. These heavily laden, double-headed holiday expresses would have made for quite a sight on this lengthy single track route. Note the local coal merchant's lorry loading from the wooden sided wagons in the siding in the left background. No. 9013, built in July 1937 as No. 3213, was based at Machynlleth shed, from where it was to be withdrawn just over two years after this picture was taken, in December 1958. The 2-6-0, which was shedded at Croes Newydd at this time, had a thirty-nine year career that lasted from January 1921 to January 1960, its final allocation being to Banbury in November 1958. The lack of space here presumably accounted for the rather complicated pointwork providing access to the short siding from both lines.

A section of the railway which seems to have been rarely photographed was the chord from Corwen round to to the Vale of Clwyd. It is shown here in this view of BR 'Standard' Class '4' No. 75054, leaving Corwen for Rhyl with the 'Welsh Chieftain Land Cruise' on 18th June 1959. The rear vehicle, a Pullman Observation coach, is just coming off the end of the iron viaduct carrying the line across the River Dee. The rest of the train was made up entirely of ex-LM&SR stock. Regular passenger services on this route had ceased in February 1953 but it remained open for goods traffic until 30th April 1962.

Leaking steam and belching forth a plume of dirty smoke, 'Dukedog' No. 9004 and Class '63xx' No. 6340 were clearly working hard as they breasted the summit at Garneddwen with the 'SO' 7.20am Pwllheli to Paddington service on 22nd August 1959. This is our third encounter with No. 9004, built in August 1938 as No. 3204 *Earl of Dartmouth*; the engine was to be withdrawn just under a year later, in June 1960.

A fine 'going-away' shot of the Festiniog Railway Society's special of 30th April 1960. This day excursion started out from Paddington behind 'County' Class 4-6-0 No. 1021 *County of Montgomery*, which hauled the train as far as Ruabon. From there, it handed over to No. 7827 *Lydham Manor* and 4-4-0 No. 9014 for the journey to Minffordd, where the proximity of the BR and Festiniog stations allowed passengers to switch from standard gauge to narrow gauge. Ifor photographed the special on its outward run, pulling away from Dolgellau station (Dolgelley up until 1960) alongside the Afon Wnion. Note the specially prepared roof-boards. The return run mirrored the westward journey. Apparently, the FR had requested the more appropriately named No. 1019 *County of Merioneth* for the main line legs of the trip but for whatever reason it was not available. The route of this attractive section of railway through Dolgellau is today buried beneath the realigned A470 road.

On 18th September 1960, a ten-coach excursion carrying reporting No. X05 was run from Pwllheli to Blackpool, especially for the autumn 'Illuminations'. The afternoon light picked out the details of the two locomotives clearly that day, a pair of Collett 0-6-0s, with No. 2214 leading No. 2204, as it threaded its way through Bontnewydd station. Both engines were based at Machynlleth at this date but No. 2204 had migrated away to the ex-Somerset & Dorset Railway shed at Templecombe by the time of its withdrawal in December 1963. No. 2214, meanwhile, was to be transferred to Shrewsbury by the end of the year (the Stephenson Locomotive Society suggest Kidderminster) and was then sent to Southern Region territory in August 1963, to Exmouth Junction shed, from where it was withdrawn in May 1965. Note that the train again appears to be made up of ex-LM&SR stock, with the possible exception of the penultimate coach.

Class '57xx' pannier tank No. 5774 of Croes Newydd shed runs off the western end of Cwm Prysor Viaduct, with a mixed consist of two coaches and two vans forming the 11.55am Bala to Blaenau Festiniog service on 3rd August 1955. The viaduct displays evidence of recent attention from the maintenance department, with a new parapet and fence, and possibly some repointing to the stonework as well. Passenger services between Bala and Blaenau Festiniog were to be withdrawn on 2nd January 1960, with goods traffic following on 27th January 1961. The leading vehicle appears to be a non-corridor coach, the first such that we have encountered on a service train in these pages.

On the same day, Ifor recorded sister engine No. 9793 heading across the viaduct in the opposite direction, with a Trawsfynydd-Bala goods. Although this was clearly a sunny day, it still failed to disguise completely the bleak nature of the terrain at this location and winter conditions can be well imagined. However, the line's very remoteness has seen much of the route remain intact and the viaduct happily still stands today. A last day special passenger train, which ran over the line on 22nd January 1961, was filmed for the BBC *Railway Roundabout* series.

Pannier tanks No's 9669 and 4617 (rear), both of Croes Newydd shed, approach Arenig with a Bala-Blaenau Festiniog freight on 21st June 1960. With passenger services having already been withdrawn, this was something of a final 'hurrah' for the line (and for Ifor's coverage of it), with this heavily laden train requiring two locomotives to take it over the mountains. The secret lies in the seven 'Presflo' cement hoppers and the two bogie bolster wagons following them, which will all be dropped off at Trawsfynydd for use in the construction of the nuclear power station, begun in July 1959 and in operation by March 1965. Shut down in 1991, rail traffic in association with its decommissioning ceased in 1997 and the last section of the line, from Blaenau Festiniog to Trawsfynydd was closed, although the track was left in place and there are currently tentative plans to reopen it as a preserved railway.

Former Cambrian Railways 0-6-0 No. 844, with British Railways' first and much-loved 'cycling lion' emblem on its tender, negotiates the picturesque gorge at Tylwch, as it approaches the station with the 9.55am Moat Lane Junction to Brecon passenger service on 19th April 1952. Built by Beyer, Peacock in October 1918 and originally Cambrian Railways No. 15, the engine had just over two years left in service with BR, being withdrawn in August 1954. The varied collection of coaching stock making up No. 844's train comprise a 'Toplight' coach, with its toplights plated over, a Collett large window Brake Third and a Collett 'Sunshine' Third.

5
MID WALES

Another of the former Cambrian '15' or 'Large Belpaire Goods' Class 0-6-0s, No. 896, leaves Tylwch with the 1.20pm passenger service from Brecon to Moat Lane Junction on 24th May 1952. The fifteen engines which constituted this class were built in three batches, in 1903 (by Robert Stephenson & Co.), and in 1908 and 1918-19 (both by Beyer, Peacock & Co.). As Cambrian No. 54, this engine was the last of the 1908 batch, all built in March of that year, but was then renumbered as No. 102 in the August. Confusingly, the final engine of the 1918-19 batch was given Cambrian Railways No. 54, becoming GWR No. 874 after Grouping. When seen here, No. 896 was working from Brecon shed but had less than a year left in service, the end coming in April 1953. As a reminder of its previous ownership, note the letters G W R showing through the worn paintwork on the tender. The fireman is taking a short breather and watching the photographer as the train glides away from the station.

'Dean Goods' No. 2452 approaches Pant-y-dwr on 24th May 1952 with the 9.45am goods from Talyllyn Junction to Moat Lane Junction. With the valley behind basking in late spring sunshine and the sun glinting off the engine's smokebox door handle, this higly evocative view shows a time and way of life now long lost. Allocated to Brecon shed and in the last five months of its working life at the time of this view, 1895-built No. 2492 was one of the sixty-two members of the class that saw service with the ROD in France during 1917-19.

The services on the Mid-Wales sector, south of Llanidloes to Brecon, were dominated by the ex-Cambrian and 'Dean Goods' 0-6-0s from the 1930s through to the early 1950s, as these photographs show. This domination was ended by the introduction of Ivatt's lightweight design 2-6-0s built first by the LM&SR and then subsequently by BR, some of which were constructed at Swindon after adaptation and modification. Just prior to that new era, No. 2408 was one of the last 'Dean Goods' still working the area when photographed by Ifor near St. Harmon with the 9.00am Talyllyn Junction to Moat Lane Junction goods on 5th July 1952. On this warm day, the driver has his sleeves rolled up as he looks towards the camera. Note the consist included a number of lime wagons at the rear, with their white-stained underframes, and one brand new steel-bodied mineral wagon in amongst the ageing wooden-bodied types, several of which show signs of being ex-private owners. In to service in November 1891, Oswestry-based No. 2408 was withdrawn in January 1953.

The highly scenic Mid Wales Railway route was undoubtedly a great loss to railway enthusiasts and photographers but meandering, as it did, through a largely sparsely populated area, loadings were light and services infrequent. Its closure was thus no surprise and it is now only through the camera lens of those such as Ifor that we can once again enjoy and appreciate some of its wild splendour and sleepy stations. No. 844, again, enters Tylwch with the 9.55am Moat Lane to Brecon train, past the small but attractive signal box, on 26th July 1952. The smokebox door numberplate looks considerably newer than the rest of the engine!

Later that same day also saw the recording of 'Dean Goods' No. 2351 with the Up 12.50pm passenger service from Builth Road to Moat Lane Junction, again near St. Harmon. This was one of the early members of the class, built in November 1884 and withdrawn in February 1953, eighteen months or so short of its seventieth birthday. Its long life can no doubt be partly attributed to the fact that it managed to avoid service with first the ROD and then the WD in both world wars. In another demonstration of the variety that could be found even with simple, short formations such as this, No. 2351's train is made up of a Collett 'high waist' Brake Composite, an ex-LM&SR Brake Third and a Collett 'high waist' Third.

The modified 'Ivatt' 2-6-0s were introduced in place of the ageing 0-6-0s. Here, No. 46514 is seen approaching Penpontbren, a mile south of Llanidloes, with the 1.20pm. Brecon to Moat Lane Junction service on 27th October 1956. This was the site of the former (admittedly, short-lived) junction with the Manchester & Milford Railway's line to Strata Florida via Llangurig, the formation of which Ifor was standing on and which was intended to connect the two places of its title by means of running rights over other companies' lines – the M&MR was only authorised to build between Llanidloes and Pencader. Construction of this line never proceeded beyond Llangurig, however, just three miles away, and only one (goods) train is known to have made even this short journey. The photograph, with imagination, could thus represent a view taken from an M&MR train waiting at the junction, had the line ever been completed throughout. The 2-6-0 was built by BR at Swindon Works in December 1952, following which it was sent to Oswestry shed where it stayed until 1965. It was withdrawn in 1966 from Carnforth.

Ivatt Class '2MT' No. 46519 approaching Pant-y-dwr with the 7.45pm Builth Wells to Moat Lane Junction train on 8th July 1959. Again Swindon-built, by BR but in February 1953, No. 46519 was also sent straight to Oswestry, from where it migrated to Machynlleth in 1963. A new allocation to Shrewsbury in early 1965 was followed by Nuneaton a few months later, before its final posting to Stoke in June 1966, from where it was withdrawn in the October. Two Collett large window coaches make up this train, the leading one, probably a Brake Composite, being in BR lined maroon livery, whilst the rear one, a 'Sunshine' Brake Third (now a Brake Second), is in crimson and cream.

A final view of one of the Ivatt 'Moguls' on the Mid Wales line, showing No. 46520 pulling away from the picturesque Pant-y-dwr station with the 2.55pm Moat Lane Junction to Brecon service on 28th May 1960. Note that Up and Down passenger trains had crossed here on this occasion, a rare busy moment in the afternoon shift for the Pant-y-dwr signalman. The locomotive's career closely matched that of sister engine No. 46519 in the previous picture: new from Swindon in February 1953 and sent to Oswestry, it also went to Machynlleth in 1963, Nuneaton in 1965 and Stoke in June 1966 but was then transferred to Northwich in October to see out a final few months of service, withdrawal taking place in May 1967. The train is made up of a Hawksworth Brake Composite – note the shape of the roof – along with a late Collett large window Brake Composite, the picture showing clearly the difference in the side profiles of Hawksworth and Collett coaches.

6
THE
MANCHESTER & MILFORD LINE

RIGHT: Had the original scheme to connect the Mid Wales Railway with the Manchester & Milford Railway, been executed, across the uplands of Plynlimon, the connection north from Strata Florida to Aberystwyth might not then have been built. Here, on 30th April 1955, 2-6-0 No. 5395, working a Carmarthen to Aberystwyth goods, was momentarily separated from its train to allow a banking engine, 'Dukedog' No. 9022, to return to Aberystwyth tender-first 'inside' it and thus to save a 'light engine' movement over this single track route.

BELOW: Previously seen No. 9013 features again, climbing the bank on its approach to Trawscoed with the 7.20am Aberystwyth to Carmarthen train on 18th June 1955.

A lovely close-up study of 4-4-0 No. 9022, this time heading north on local passenger duties. The engine has paused with its two-coach train, the 2.40pm Carmarthen to Aberystwyth service, at the rural but attractively situated Caradog Falls Halt on 18th June 1955. Constructed in December 1938 from the frames of 'Bulldog' No. 3436 and replacing 'Duke' No. 3278 from which it also received parts, No. 9022 was allocated to Machynlleth shed at this date, from where it would be withdrawn in August 1957. Situated a little way north of Strata Florida, Caradog Falls Halt was opened on 5th September 1932, serving the nearby hamlet of Tynygraig. Behind the train can be seen the north portal of the 86-yards long Tynygraig Tunnel.

'Collett' 0-6-0 No. 2224 heads north above Trawscoed with a short morning freight, the 7.30am Aberystwyth-Carmarthen goods, on 18th June 1955. As well as the brake van, the train comprises two larger capacity steel mineral wagons and two milk tank wagons; the latter will be from the dairy at Pont Llanio. A war-time build at Swindon in Sepetmber 1940, No. 2224 was allocated to Aberystwyth shed at the time of this view but had moved east to St. Phillips Marsh at Bristol by the time it was withdrawn in September 1963, a working life of just twenty-three years.

Another glimpse of Caradog Falls Halt but looking in the opposite direction, with No. 9013 just departing at the head of the 9.15am 'SO' Aberystwyth to Carmarthen train on 19th July 1955. Note the fire-irons resting on the coal in No. 9013's tender. The fresh ballast indicates that track here had clearly had recent attention from the permanent way department. The leading coach appears to be an old ex-LM&SR vehicle – note how the division between the carmine and the cream comes half-way up the waist panels.

No. 9013 was clearly very familiar with the M&MR line, featuring here once again piloting 2-6-0 No. 5333 of Tyseley (84E) shed near Strata Florida on Wednesday 27th July 1955. The working is an Aberystwyth to Swansea School Excursion, which No. 5333 was presumably pressed in to hauling having previously arrived at the Cambrian line terminus with a train from Birmingham. The first two coaches again appear to be ex-LM&SR stock.

Excursions over Cambrian lines could be quite heavy and lengthy trains, with a typical example being shown here. No 7826 *Longworth Manor* and No. 7825 *Lechlade Manor* surmount the bank near Llanrhystyd Road, the first station south from Aberystwyth, with the twelve coaches forming a returning 'Swansea and District Holiday Express' on 3rd August 1959.

Up and Down goods trains cross at Strata Florida on 23rd September 1961. Collet 0-6-0 No. 2255 departs down the 1 in 45 bank towards Aberystwyth with cement 'Presflos' and milk tank wagons, whilst an unidentified classmate waits for the 'off' with a southbound train. Oddly, there is a sheeted van at the rear of this train, behind the brake van, so perhaps some shunting has been interrupted by the passing of No. 2255. The station was as isolated as it appears, Strata Florida Abbey being nearly three miles away, whilst the nearest village, Pontrhydfendigaid, was also over a mile distant.

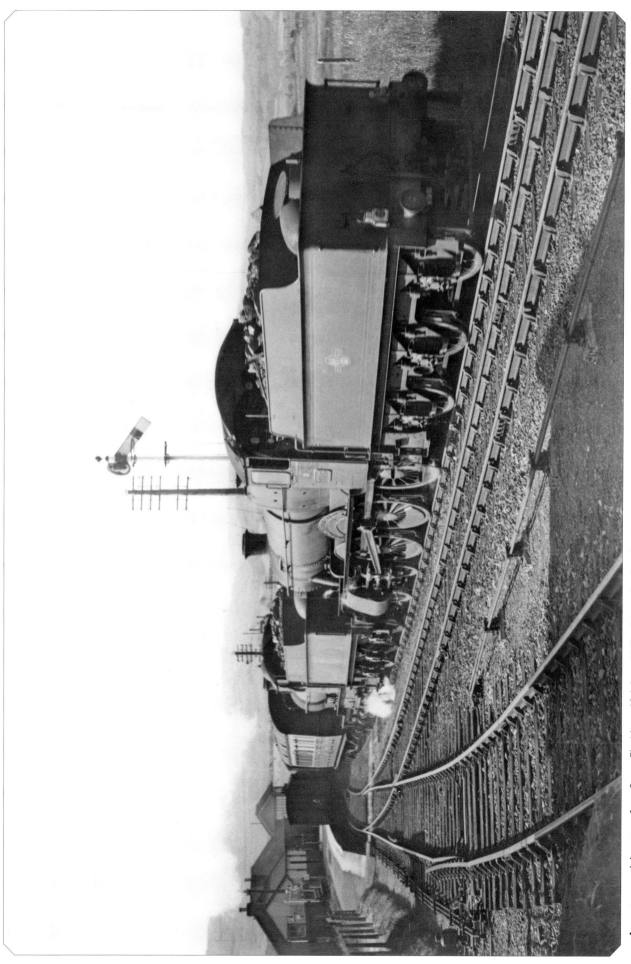

A most unusual departure from Strata Florida on 13th June 1959, with a pair of tender-first locomotives doubling up on an excursion. No. 7823 *Hook Norton Manor* and 4-4-0 No. 9017 were hauling a Lampeter to Barmouth excursion of nine carriages down to Aberystwyth, where the haulage arrangements were able to be regularised. The day had begun with a smokebox first trip south to pick up the excursionists at Lampeter, where the locomotives then ran round their train to begin the journey back north. Tender first in to Aberystwyth then became right way facing for departure. Strata Florida was a regular passing point and a southbound goods was again being crossed.

We return to the Cambrian main line again for this second view of the Lampeter to Barmouth excursion, now heading north towards Dovey Junction behind No. 7823 *Hook Norton Manor*, the 'Dukedog' having been dropped off at Aberystwyth, no longer required on the easily graded northern part of the journey. Ifor took this second view of the train as it passed through Bow Street, the first station out from Aberystwyth, which was closed on 14th June 1965. However, a new station is scheduled to be opened here by March 2020, funding haviung been secured by the Welsh Government from the Department for Transport. Bow Street has grown since the station was closed and is also now the home of Aberystwyth University's Gogerddan campus. The station will be on a new site just to the south of the original, which is now occupied by a builders' merchants. No. 7823 was withdrawn from Tyseley shed in July 1964. The leading coach is a Hawksworth Brake Third (now running as a Brake Second), whilst the following two look like ex-LM&SR vehicles again.

7
SALOPIAN INTERLUDE

RIGHT: In the early 1930s, Ifor made at least four visits to the Shropshire & Montgomeryshire Railway, which by this time was in a parlous state as the photographs show. The line formed part of Colonel Holman F. Stephens light railway empire but he was seriously ill by the date of this first visit and died in 1931. Three ex-LB&SCR Stroudley 'Terrier' 0-6-0 tanks were acquired by Stephens from the Admiralty after the First World War, No's 638, 681 and 683. The latter became S&MR No. 7 *Hecate* (the third of Stephens' engines to carry this name) but had just been laid aside when seen here at Kinnerley on 7th June 1930, where it was slowly dismantled for spares and then sold for scrap.

BELOW: The much photographed and well documented *Gazelle*, seen at Kinnerley on 2nd July 1931, survived the line's demise to be preserved.

A general view of Kinnerley shed on 7th June 1930, showing *Gazelle*, two petrol railcars and a coach stored in the siding on the right, whilst the boiler of *Thisbe*, an ex-L&SWR 'Ilfracombe Goods' Class 0-6-0, can be seen on the left. Stephens bought seven of these ancient but versatile engines in total, between 1910 and 1918, three of which were for the S&MR: L&SWR No's 0283 (bought 1910), 0300 and 0324 (both 1913); the '0' had been added when they were placed on the duplicate list, their numbers having been taken by newer locomotives. On the S&MR, they became No's 6 *Thisbe*, 5 *Pyramus* and 3 *Hesperus* respectively. The cab on the coal stage is also from *Thisbe* and probably the tender too, just glimpsed in the centre background. *Thisbe*'s boiler was life expired and the engine was out of use at this time. However, in October 1930, it was to be rebuilt using the boiler from No. 5 *Pyramus* and returned to traffic, continuing in service until laid aside in September 1935. It was finally broken up here in May 1937. The site of Kinnerley station and engine shed is still clearly defined today but nothing of the railway remains apart from the bridge over the line at the east end.

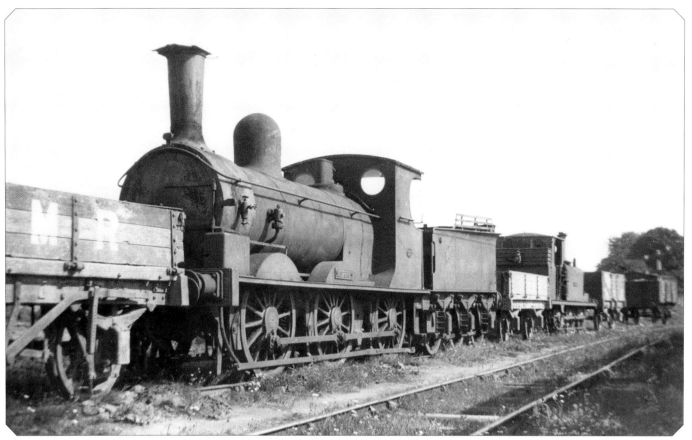

Another of the 'Ilfracombe Goods', No. 3 *Hesperus* at Kinnerley on 18th August 1932, with one of the 'Terriers' in the background. *Hesperus* was the last of the three ex-L&SWR engines to work on the S&MR, hauling a weekly stone train to and from Criggion Quarry in 1938-39. Finally expiring in May 1939, the engine was broken up in the sidings at Shrewsbury in November 1941. Meanwhile, the Shropshire & Montgomeryshire Railway was about to be taken over by the War Department and was to enjoy a further lease of life until 1960.

The remains of the 0-4-2 tank *Severn*, partly dismantled and sat amidst general decay and upheaval at Kinnerley on 18th August 1932. Stephens had purchased the engine from Griff Collieries in Warwickshire in 1911. However, its history prior to that is uncertain. It may have been an 0-4-2 tender engine built for the St. Helens Canal & Railway Company circa 1853, as their No. 23 *Hero*. Passing in to L&NWR stock when the SHC&R was absorbed in 1864, it became No. 1389 but was sold almost immediately in 1865 to J. Cross & Co., who rebuilt it as a tank engine and sold it on in 1869 to the Bristol Port Railway & Pier Company, their No. 2. It was sold again in 1890, possibly to Griff Collieries, when the BPR&P Co. was jointly taken over by the Midland and Great Western railways. However, it may instead have been an inside cylinder 0-4-2 saddle tank named *Crewe*, built by Bury, Courts & Kennedy in the 1840s for the L&NWR and sold to Griff Collieries in 1871. Whichever, Stephens promptly named it *Hecate* but then changed it to *Severn* in 1916. It had been laid aside by the S&MR in the early 1920s and subsequently robbed for parts for other engines.

ABOVE: Ifor's caption on the reverse of this print reads '*The boilers of* Daphne, Dido *and* Hecate *at Kinnerley*' and was also taken on his visit of 18th August 1932. However, only two boilers can actually be seen and it is probably the case that he was unsure as to whether the one on the left was from *Daphne* or *Dido*. The boiler to the fore is that of *Hecate*, the 'Terrier' 0-6-0 we saw a little earlier, shortly after it had first been laid aside. The one on the left is from *Dido*, another 'Terrier' 0-6-0T, LB&SCR No. 683, which was laid aside around the same time and had also been dismantled for parts, to keep *Daphne*, the third of the S&MR's 'Terriers', in operation. This was successful to the extent that *Daphne* was sold back to the Southern Railway in 1939, as a source of spares for their own fleet of 'Terriers', finally being scrapped at Eastleigh in 1949. Note the rake of private owner wagons behind, waiting to head back up to Criggion Quarry, which is still in operation today.

BELOW: The former Royal Saloon at Kinnerley on 18th August 1932, lettered as S&MR No. 1A, with a Third Class coach alongside.

BELOW: A final view of Kinnerley shed on 14th April 1933, with ex-LM&SR No. 8108, bought in 1930 and No. 8182, bought in 1931, standing in front. An upsurge in quarry traffic in 1930, brought on by the construction of a major new road in Lancashire, prompted the S&MR to buy three locomotives from the LM&SR, two in 1930 and one in 1932, all ex-L&NWR 'Coal Engine' 0-6-0s, to supplement the 'Ilfracombe Goods'. All three survived to be taken over with the line by the Military on 1st September 1939 and were kept going throughout the war by a combination of Crewe Works and army repairs. Falling in to the hands of the Western Region of BR in 1949, they suffered the ignominy of being scrapped at Swindon in 1950.

A single visit to the Bishops Castle Railway on 29th June 1932, when apparently no services were in operation, resulted in this image of the 0-6-0 *Carlisle* at the terminus. Built originally as an 0-6-0 saddle tank by Kitson & Co. in 1868 for the Carlisle-based contractor Thomas Nelson, the engine was acquired from an unknown source in 1895. The BCR opened for traffic in 1866, as part of an intended route from Craven Arms to Montgomery but the money ran out after Bishops Castle was reached and it was never completed. A receiver was appointed in 1867, the company then being run in receivership for the rest of its existence, closure finally taking place with the suspension of operations on 20th April 1935.

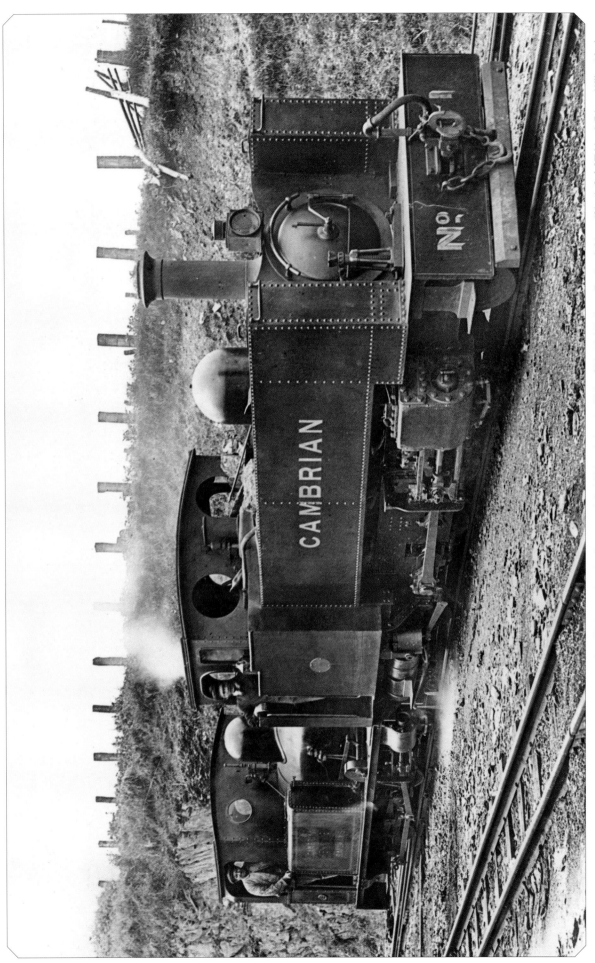

A 'collected' view by a well known contemporary photographer, W. Leslie Good, taken circa July 1921 and showing Vale of Rheidol Railway Davies & Metcalf-built 2-6-2T No. 1 *Edward VII*, with the smaller 2-4-0 No. 3 *Rheidol* behind, at the Devil's Bridge terminus. The Cambrian had widened the cabs of both engines and note the differing lettering styles. It is thought that D&M studied the drawings of the Lynton & Barnstaple Railway's Manning, Wardle-built 2-6-2Ts, hence the similarity between the designs. No's 1 and 2 were built by D&M in 1902 and became GWR No's 1212 and 1213 respectively after Grouping. After some initial work by Swindon to improve them, both were scrapped by the GWR (D&M never built any more locomotives after the VoR tanks, which perhaps tells its own story!). VoR No's 7 & 8 were built new in 1923 to replace them, Swindon basically taking the design, adding a larger, more efficient Belpaire boiler, new GWR pattern cylinders and outside Walschaert's gear. Later in 1924, another one was built to the Swindon design and given No 1213, an act which has since led to persistent rumours that it is a rebuild of the original D&M-built machine. No. 3, Bagnall Works No. 1497 of 1896, was allocated GWR No. 1198 but was also quickly withdrawn, in July 1924.

8
NARROW GAUGE

RIGHT: Corris Railway No. 3 or, by this time, more accurately, an amalgam of No's 1, 2 and 3, only had a few months of passenger operation still left, before the service was withdrawn by the GWR on 1st January 1931, although freight services (and No. 3) were to continue until 1948. The locomotive is seen awaiting departure from the terminus adjacent to the main line station at Machynlleth, with a passenger train for Aberllefenni on 16th August 1930. Ifor's visit was prescient, the GWR having taken over the Corris just twelve days earlier. The engine is still in service today, as Talyllyn Railway No. 3 *Sir Haydn*.

BELOW: The day previously, Ifor had photographed Talyllyn No. 2 *Dolgoch* at Tywyn, albeit with neither name nor number anywhere to be seen.

ABOVE: Ifor photographed TR No. I *Talyllyn* in steam at Pendre, possibly on the same day and again without a name or number to be seen.

BELOW: The Welsh Highland Railway's Hunslet Engine Co., 1906-built 2-6-2T *Russell*, travelling bunker first through the highly picturesque Aberglaslyn Pass, with a Portmadoc to Beddgelert and Dinas Junction train on 7th August 1933. The line closed in 1937 but was re-opened between 1997 and 2011, whilst *Russell* survived an eventful subsequent existence to be restored and today can be seen on occasion working through the gorge once again.

North Wales has an enviable record for preserving and re-opening many of its narrow gauge lines, with the Corris Railway the latest to make significant progress after many years of patient negotiations. However, one of the most significant losses was the 4ft gauge Dinorwic Quarries Railway, more commonly known as the Padarn Railway, which joined the slate mines of Llanberis with Port Dinorwic, seven miles away on the coast facing the Menai Strait. On 26th May 1959, Ifor photographed the Hunslet Engine Co. (Works No. 410 of 1886) 0-6-0T *Amalthaea* leaving Port Dinorwic with a train of 4ft gauge transporter wagons loaded with 2ft gauge slate empties for the quarry. Although the main line was laid to the wider gauge, the lines within the quarry and at the port were all 2ft gauge. Originally named *Pandora*, the engine was renamed in May 1909 and lasted in service until closure of the Padarn Railway, on 27th October 1961, slate being sent by road thereafter, until the quarry itself closed in 1969. *Amalthaea* was scrapped on site at Gilfachddu, Llanberis in August 1963, whilst the south-eastern end of the main line has been relaid as the 2½ mile-long 2ft gauge Llanberis Lake Railway.

ABOVE: The Port Dinorwic terminus of the Padarn Railway main line was at the incline head, where a rake of transporter wagons were awaiting return to the quarries on 25th September 1956. Note the 2ft/4ft gauge combination allowed for two rakes of narrow gauge slate wagons to be loaded side by side, four per transporter, whilst there was only one wagon brake per train.

BELOW: The first of the Hunslet Engine Co. 0-6-0 tanks, *Dinorwic* (Works No. 310 of 1882) heads west at Erw Fforch late in the afternoon of 31st July 1957, with a loaded train for Port Dinorwic, which included the pay coach on the rear. *Dinorwic*'s fate mirrored that of *Amalthaea*.

The other important loss as regards the quarry lines of North Wales was the Penrhyn Quarry Railway of 1801, a 2ft gauge line which ran from the slate quarries at Bethesda to Port Penrhyn, on the Menai Strait immediately to the north of Bangor. Penrhyn Railway 0-4-0 saddle tank *Blanche*, seen in sylvan surroundings near Felin Hen whilst *en route* from Port Penrhyn to Bethesda with a train of empty waggons on 10th October 1956, was another Hunslet Engine Co. product, Works No. 589 of 1893. A steam engine was first used on a short section of the railway in 1875, which was then subsequently rebuilt in 1879-79 to allow locomotives to work the line throughout. Passenger trains for quarrymen were also operated but these had ceased on 10th February 1951. The last slate train over the main line ran on 24th July 1962 but some of the lines within the quarry itself continued in use until early 1965. The track on the main line was bought for re-use by the Festiniog Railway and lifted in 1965. Many of the Penrhyn's extensive fleet of locomotives survived to be preserved, some on display at various museums but a number are still working, *Blanche* and her sister *Linda* (consecutive HE Works No. 590 of 1893) transferred to the Festiniog Railway in December 1963 and July 1962 respectively, where both have since been rebuilt as 2-4-0 saddle tanks (in 1970 and 1972).

A second view of *Blanche* taken around ten months later, on 31st July 1957, at Tregarth Loop with a train of empties from Port Penrhyn bound for Bethesda. The line was around six miles in length and headed south from Port Penrhyn, initially running parallel to the standard gauge Penrhyn Branch built by the L&NWR which also served the port. Near Glasynfryn it then crossed over the ex-L&NWR Bethesda Branch, which made its way to the town whilst the narrow gauge line was bound for the quarry. None of these lines remain today, so this delightful view of Ifor's serves both to remind us of the delights of a warm summer afternoon in the North Wales countryside waiting for the occasional train to pass – which in fact appears to have been stopped by its driver and posed for the photographer – whilst also neatly rounding off this short but sweet tour of the Cambrian region, in the company of a talented but modest practitioner of his art.